The Shoe Box

WALKING *in the* SPIRIT

PATSY CLAIRMONT

W PUBLISHING GROUP™

www.wpublishinggroup.com

A Division of Thomas Nelson, Inc.
www.ThomasNelson.com

To Amy Miller,
who always puts her best foot forward.

The Shoe Box
© 2003 by Patsy Clairmont

Published by W Publishing Group, a Division of Thomas
Nelson, Inc., P.O. Box 141000, Nashville, Tennessee 37214.

Scripture quotations in this book are from *The New King
James Version* © 1984 by Thomas Nelson, Inc. unless specified
otherwise. Other Scripture quotations are from:
The Holy Bible, New International Version (NIV) © 1973, 1984
by International Bible Society, used by permission of Zondervan
Publishing House; *New American Standard Bible*® (NASB)
© 1960, 1977, 1995 by the Lockman Foundation;
The King James Version (KJV).

ISBN 0-8499-1796-4

Printed in the United States of America
03 04 05 06 PHX 5 4 3 2

Contents

When the shoe fits, we girls are like
Cinderella—we're having a ball.

Steppin' Out

If you want to buy me a gift (as if), don't buy me shoes. Yep, I said don't. Instead, give me a gift coupon to purchase my own footwear. You see, I'm really picky. Besides, I love toting home shoe boxes. I feel so, so . . . womanly. And it tickles me to know the fun shoe choices tucked inside will enliven my wardrobe. Even after the boxes are empty, they become the perfect spot to store stuff. Good stuff like pictures, gloves, memos, scarves, receipts, and even outdated shoes that I'm waiting to come back into style.

Like that's going to happen. Oh, some looks do go full circle, but the new version always has a fashion adjustment that dates the ones I've tenaciously held onto.

Shoes are addictive. I think that's because they come in so many flavors—mules, pumps, flats, spikes, wedges, platforms, etc. And it's a good thing they do because the wrong shoes can wreck a girl's outfit, not to mention her feet and her attitude. Imagine Martha Stewart in strapless pumps spreading fertilizer over her garden while announcing, "It's a good thing." Nah, it's not going to happen. What about Laura Bush attending a White House news conference wearing a classic navy suit accessorized with iridescent-studded motorcycle boots? Tacky. Or imagine the Queen of England horseback riding in her house slippers. Uh-oh, call the royal shoe patrol. Yep, shoes definitely leave loud statements.

But shoes aren't the only things talking. I remember a declaration my feet made when I attempted to hoof the length of the D/FW International Airport in high heels. I know, I know, what was I thinking? Obviously I wasn't. Less than halfway through the terminal I thought I was terminal. My feet were pulsating like hot dogs on a spit. After developing a painful limp, I pried my now-swollen tootsies out of my heels and finished the hike to my gate stocking-footed. That did garner a few stares, but that's not the sort of footwear news I want to make.

A kickier statement is made when, prior to the Miss America pageant, the beauty contestants participate in a shoe parade. How fun is that? The young women, wearing elaborate outfits, perch on the backs of convertibles, and as they cruise by, the spectators yell, "Show us your shoes!" The bevy of beauties lift their feet to show off the most outrageous shoes you've ever seen. Some are arrayed in huge feathers or trees (yes, trees a foot high). Other shoes are jeweled, sequined, striped, and polka-dotted. After the parade, the shoes are showcased with the contestants' gowns.

Now, while I have a slew of eclectic footwear, I'm not sure any of it would qualify for a parade. I seem to be the queen of scuffs, gouges, and fractured heels. Besides, I don't have even one pair with a tree sprouting out of them. Although I do have a darling pair of slides with embroidered palm trees and golden monkeys. Say, maybe I could be in a parade.

When the shoe fits both our outfit and our feet, we girls are like a beauty queen or Cinderella—we're having a ball.

Have you noticed that men tend not to be as footish? At least my hubby, Les, isn't. He owns two pairs of shoes, and he can't figure out for the life of him why he bought the second pair. When in high school, he chose to spray-paint his white bucks rather than purchase additional shoes. But he varied the hues so many times, including gold for the prom, that the shoes finally crackled like land fissures after an earthquake. So you can imagine Les's confusion over why I would need several—okay, okay, more than several—pairs of shoes.

Les and I went on an Alaskan cruise recently, and he wanted to take out extra life insurance because he was certain my footwear alone would sink the ship. Men just don't get it.

Actually, I have trouble explaining it myself, but life offers such a kaleidoscope of challenges, and I love to be foot-ready so I can step out in style, whether it's lunch with a friend (flats), a loop around the park (sneakers), attending a conference (heels), shuffling through the house (slippers), or dinner with Les (one of the above). So it seems reasonable to me that I need a healthy collection of footgear.

While Scripture doesn't endorse personal loans for shoe fetishes, it does address our daily walk and the importance of taking the right path. So what shall it profit a woman to be dazzling in her sequined heels only to be on the wrong side of town while the party's happening?

I appreciate assurance that I'm using the right map, and I despise discovering six exits too late that I have to pivot and trod back over old territory. Unfortunately, I have to do that a lot because directions make me dizzy. Even when I'm sporting the latest hiking boots, I'm clueless as to which direction is southwest or northeast. I was born compassless. All the more reason to keep my holy "map" of God's Word before me.

Join me now as we lift the lid on our shoe boxes, don the contents, then walk, boogie, jog, stroll, and meander through our day, securing our direction and delighting in our shoe wardrobe. Along the way we will do our best to find a good fit by aligning our heart with our footpath. We'll be concentrating on the path set before us in Galatians 5:22–23: "But the fruit of the Spirit is love, joy, peace, patience, kindness, goodness, faithfulness, gentleness and self-control." Now that's a yellow brick road worthy to be trod upon by dazzling Dorothy shoes.

So c'mon, girlfriends, slide into your favorite footwear, gather up your shoe boxes, and let's step into high fashion and toe-tapping truth in style. Show me your shoes!

It won't be how many steps we take in our spectator pumps—some of us will live longer than others—but the quality of our inner lives that leaves indelible footprints behind.

Flippin' the Lid

In the opening chapter, I mentioned items we could store in a vacated shoe box, but I left out a few creative uses you might not have considered.

My older brother, Don, was a preemie, but unlike today, with our teams of medical specialists and preemie wards to assist newborns, my nervous parents had to take their infant son home to nurture him. Because he was so fragile, my mom swaddled him and tucked him inside a boot box on a pint-sized pillow. That way she could take care of her household chores and still have him within eyeshot, as she and the box moved from room to room. I guess that was Mom's version of a portable crib.

On cold winter days, Mom heated the oven and left the oven door ajar to warm the kitchen so her precious cargo in the boot box, propped on a nearby chair, would stay toasty warm.

Imagine tucking the first fruit of your womb inside a shoe box. How inventive.

Speaking of fruit, Don gave Mom plenty of opportunity to grow spiritual fruit as she cared for him because he wasn't interested in eating. She had to display tons of patience and gentleness to nudge Don to take enough nourishment so he could, in time, grow out of his boot box and into a big boy's bed.

While my dad's shoe box became a bed, my friend's dad's shoe box held bread. Singer, songwriter, and friend Babbie Mason told me of a difficult journey her parents took in which their shoe boxes became picnic baskets.

Babbie's parents, who were African-American, lived in the deep South in the 1940s but had been encouraged by family to move North for jobs and greater personal freedoms. Even though they wanted to make the journey, her parents knew it could be chancy for African-Americans to travel so far from home. But concerned that poverty would rule their existence if they didn't, they packed up and headed for Michigan.

Babbie's mom prepared meals and packed them in towel-lined shoe boxes to avoid the prejudices or potential threat of eating in restaurants. They drove at night to draw less attention to themselves during this racially tense time and then stopped in African-American neighborhoods in towns along the way to ask around for some folks who could rent a sleeping room in their home. After days of patiently planned travel, the brave family made it safely to their new home.

Now I want to flip the lid on my last shoe box. A ministry called The Samaritan's Purse conducts a loving outreach called Operation Christmas Child to benefit the world's poor children.

My young friend, six-year-old Christian (Sheila Walsh's son), filled a shoe box with items for a boy his age in an impoverished country. Christian lovingly tucked in a toothbrush, washcloth, soap, candy, pencils, notepads, Band-Aids, small toys, and even a pair of sunglasses. Get this, in 2001, five million shoe boxes like the one Christian packed were sent to ninety-five countries as children blessed other children.

The next time you lift a shoe box lid, remember that the shoes inside represent our walk through this world. And remember, it won't be how many steps we take in our spectator pumps—some of us will live longer than others—but the quality of our inner lives that leaves indelible footprints behind.

*I think stepping into God's love would cause
us to step out of our spiritual baby booties
and right into big girl's shoes.*

Baby Booties

LOVE

See Granny. See Granny grin. See Granny leap into the air and click her heels!

On June 8, 2000, I leapt into the stratosphere and almost put my sacroiliac out of whack when I became Nana to Justin Robert Clairmont. One glance of my grandson's brand-spankin'-new little toes, and my heart turned to Silly Putty and my stature shot heavenward. The cushion of grandma-glee I was walking on elevated me.

I had no idea grandmotherhood would be so, well, invigorating. I definitely have picked up my pace since that little darling sprouted on our family tree.

I realized, having birthed two sons, that new

life was life-changing, but I found becoming a nana was a futuristic kick. Having a grandchild is like a promissory note with compounded interest. It goes deep into the marrow of dry bones, replenishing them. Why, I became almost aerobic.

I was barely twenty (by twelve days) when I tied baby booties on my firstborn son, Marty. My mother, crochet-woman extraordinaire, whipped up a rainbow assortment of tiny booties for Marty in colors to match an array of outfits showered on us by well-wishers.

Before long Marty's feet were cramped, and his toes were tied up in the booties' threads, suggesting he was ready to move on to big boy shoes. Phooey. Oh, I know that's how it should be, but, golly, I would have loved to savor a little more infancy time. You know, those moments when babies still nuzzle and coo (and take multiple naps).

I would wait nine years before I heard more baby sounds and had the thrill of slipping another set of blue booties over pink toes. This time it was for Jason, our younger son. Mom again came to the rescue with her magic needles, allowing Jason to follow the booties-galore tradition of his big brother. Then Jason grew into high-topped walking shoes that all too soon would be replaced by high top (stinky) tennis shoes.

These three baby boys—Justin, Martin, and Jason—wiggled into my heart with their tiny toes and button noses bringing gurgles, giggles, and love.

I don't think anything is more appealing to a woman than love, whether it comes wrapped up in a blanket needing our nurturing touch or we're wrapped up in a loved one's hug, delighting in that embrace.

When my grandson turned two, I was away on a ten-day trip. Once I returned, I made a beeline over to see him. Just as I entered his home, Justin turned the hallway corner and spotted me. He let out an ear-piercing squeal as he ran full speed into my outstretched arms. We both giggled with delight at the joy of being together again. I've replayed that scene in my mind many times, and it serves as a sweet reminder of the blessing of mutual love. My husband was pleased to have me home as well, but nary a squeal came forth from his lips, and I'm grateful he didn't cast his two-hundred-plus-pound body up into my arms.

Of course, love can sometimes trip us up. Take my friend Cindy. When she was nine months pregnant, she decided to take her toddler with her for a last-fling shopping spree before her new little one arrived. (Probably needed to buy baby booties.) As she dressed for the occasion, she chose to wear her favorite pair of shoes—okay, the only pair she could squeeze her swollen tootsies into. She loved those shoes. The only problem was one of them had started to fall apart, with the sole coming off where the bottom of the shoe was tacked to the shoe's front.

Cindy rolled herself out of her car and then pulled the stroller from the backseat. With a flick of her foot, she hit the pedal that should have sprung the stroller open. It did, but Cindy's flapping shoe-front caught in the device, and the stroller wheeled forward with Cindy struggling to remove her foot. Next thing she knew, she was on her back in the mall's parking lot. *Hello, I've fallen and can't get up!* was her first thought, I'm sure.

Now, when Cindy tells the story, at this point, she says she "popped up" quickly, but you and I know that she was more like the sea rolling in large waves as she worked to stand up. She glanced around to make sure no one but her toddler had witnessed the incident. Then she moved forward with purpose—toward the shoe store, as a matter of fact.

I haven't stepped out in the same way Cindy has, but I have found learning to love is a steppin' out process—stepping out of me to extend myself to others in meaningful ways. If I don't purpose to extricate myself from my busyness and preoccupation with my own tangle of thoughts, I miss priceless opportunities to invest lovingly in those around me. However, my grandson, Justin, keeps me on a short rein. If my eyes begin to drift away from his to look across the room while he's talking, he emphatically states, "No, me, Nana, me!" I believe our relationship with others rescues us from drowning in our self-absorbed tendencies.

In my mid-twenties I was in the throes of struggling to become a healthier person when a friend told me, "Patsy, you need to get a job." I was floored with her assessment because I was fragile emotionally and physically. If she had suggested I needed counseling or medication, that would have seemed reasonable, but a job? Why, I could barely handle my daily chores. Then she risked telling me, "You spend too much time thinking about yourself. It's no wonder your nervous disposition is so frazzled, your faith so weak, and your world so small. Purposeful work can fill your thoughts with productive activity and give your body's energy something to do besides support your insecurities."

That was hard to hear and even more difficult to put into practice. I was in the habit of constantly scrutinizing my own body: how I was feeling, what I was thinking, and what I was doing. My friend startled me with her honesty, but what she said rang true somewhere deep within me. So I began to reach out more to others.

One way I did that was to open a small bookstore in my home. Folks would stop in to make a purchase, and I would help them to select books suited to their needs, which meant I had to be well-read and also attentive to their struggles. That helped to get my mind off myself, and I was pleased to find out later how my recommended selections had blessed others' lives. Of course, being a woman given to extremes, I then had to learn not to let my well-purposed efforts become another self-consuming activity.

My frank friend cared enough to tell me the truth, but being honest even with loving intentions can be risky and could cost you a friendship.

Especially if the friend isn't in a place to hear your heart, if she doesn't feel safe in your shared relationship, or if she's unable to face the truth about herself without shattering. Truth out of season can be damaging. Well-timed words can serve as the catalyst that promotes healing and maturity. Scripture puts it this way: "A word fitly spoken is like apples of gold in settings of silver" (Proverbs 25:11). Being selective with one's words shows wisdom and maturity.

Love is costly (ask Jesus). Financially, emotionally, physically, relationally, and spiritually one could go bankrupt loving folks (if one didn't have boundaries). Even with boundaries it takes time, dedication, forgiveness, and tenacity to be a lover of people. Why, some days I have trouble loving myself, especially as I grow older.

As the years add up, one's physical topography can change dramatically. We don't just lose agility, but our body's tone loosens, stockpiling into a series of chins, waist wads, and leg lumps. Those are adorable features on babies yet so unwanted on grownups.

My family has overheard me more than once trying to coax my mirrored reflection to "work with me" as I cover, tuck, and disguise as much of the fallen terrain as possible. Turtlenecks are a great storage place to tuck extra chins. (Where does one tuck eye droops?) I find the in-the-face reality of fading youth disconcerting, and I'm not alone. I can't tell you how many women I meet who refuse even to have their picture taken with family. One family shared with me that at the passing of a relative they found she had cut herself out of all her photographs.

Many of us need to reaffirm our internal and eternal value. If I don't have a measure of tender regard and compassion for myself, how will I lovingly interact with you? I can only give others what I have, and if I'm full of personal contempt, even my best offering will be tinged with my own ill will.

Without the giving and receiving of love the human spirit will shrivel and die. It's every bit as necessary to life as oxygen, if not more so. In fact, I've heard that neglected babies die when no one holds them, strokes their little brows, and whispers words of love.

Ah, there is yet another love, the holy love of a heavenly Father for His earthly child. His pure love provides us with a sense of safety and self and prepares us to love others more fully.

I wish all of us could grasp the deep pleasure God takes in us. I think stepping into God's love would cause us to step out of our spiritual baby booties and right into big girl's shoes. What do you think?

STEPPING INTO LOVE

Great peace have those who love Your law, and nothing causes them to stumble. (Psalm 119:165)

He has shown you, O man, what is good. And what does the LORD require of you? To act justly and to love mercy and to walk humbly with your God. (Micah 6:8 NIV)

Owe nothing to anyone except to love one another; for he who loves his neighbor has fulfilled the law. (Romans 13:8 NASB)

SHOESTRINGS: TYING UP LOVE

Your love, O God, compassionately rescues us from a narrow existence. Enlarge Your territory within us. Move into the chaotic corners of our hearts with Your presence. Tutor us to be lavish with Your love. Grow us up as we walk in Your ways. Amen.

I'm grateful that the Lord has sent
an entourage of courageous women
to jeté through my life.

Ballet Slippers

JOY

The ballet days of my youth continue to hold fond fodder for my mind. On Saturday mornings, when I was ten years old, I would bounce out of bed, dress, grab my ballet slippers, and walk a half-mile to my ballet class. Trust me, it takes a lot for me to bounce in the morning, but dance motivated me.

Truth be told, I still have my ballet slippers. Does it seem silly that I've saved them all these years? I think I believed that one day I would use them again. But now my years have stockpiled into a stack higher than I'm tall. Besides, at this point in my journey, I couldn't fit one of those tiny slippers on my bunion much less my puffy feet. Yet when I glance into the guest bedroom and see those sweet slippers hanging on the wall, I have two responses. First, I have a moment of reverie, and then I'm reminded to keep dancing. Oh, not a pirouette (I'm dizzy enough) or even a grand jeté (midair leap—ouch), but to move through my remaining days with a toe-tapping melody of joy.

My friend Luci Swindoll has reminded me repeatedly that every day contains reasons to be joyful. She is seventy years old, and honey, Luci doesn't just move across a room—she literally waltzes, sometimes bee-bops (honest), and often moonwalks (her preference). Whether on a hot-air-balloon photographic safari over the Serengeti, touring the Taj Mahal, visiting the destitute in Ghana, taking a headcount of penguins in Antarctica, or coaxing a flower in her garden into bloom, this woman knows how to step out and embrace life.

Some days, like Luci, I really get that joy stuff. I enter into the tasks set before me with gusto while my heart hums (at first I thought it was indigestion). But other days I'm too full of sadness or too full of myself (now that's indigestion), or too overwhelmed with responsibilities to have much space for joy. On those days, I limp through the hours unaware of any dance steps that might return me to the joyful path. I'm grateful that the Lord has sent an entourage of courageous women to jeté through my life and help me see what I almost missed.

Women like Luci and women in the midst of crisis and tragedy have taught me that life's dance of joy can be done in the shadows as well as the sunshine. Joy actually sparkles in darkness, and like heavenly fireworks, joy doesn't require daylight and cloudless skies. In fact, the illuminating wonder of joy dazzles with contrast. Its display causes grown women to lace up their toeshoes and join the celebration.

Recently a ballerina approached my book table at a conference. I knew she was a ballerina because the rhythm of her indomitable dancing spirit was so palpable. When this young woman, named Sheila, neared me, in a soft yet steady voice, she announced that she was in stage-four cancer.

I was so impressed that Sheila had the strength, interest, and determination to press past her disease to fellowship with others. Who would have blamed her if she had hung up her dancing shoes and stayed in bed? Certainly not me. But Sheila was determined as long as breath was in her body to dance on and, when her breathing stopped, to pirouette into glory. No retirement for her ballet slippers.

Joy is durable. It holds up under hardship and often is showcased in life's distresses. Joy is contagious as well and causes even the halt to stand on tiptoes and twirl.

My friend Shirley just underwent a double hip replacement. The doctor had never performed this procedure before, so Shirley was the talk of the hospital. But she wasn't the conversation topic just because of her radical operation. Her unusual level of joy, which seemed to buoy her through her pain, placed her center stage with the nurses and aides. Her joy didn't remove her pain, but it supported her courageous heart. Nurses were vying to have her as their patient. Imagine that.

When her husband, Marv, approached her room following surgery, he heard gales of laughter. A nurse who was exiting the room looked at him and said, "If you know this woman, you're a lucky guy." He agreed. Joy is winsome.

Last month Shirley had both knees replaced. She called me the other day to say she was praying for me. For me. This gal deserves several curtain calls, for she characterizes ballet's signature of elegance and grace. She would be the first to say joy is a Jesus song that He willingly sings into the human spirit.

Shirley is choosing to don dancing shoes, regardless of her condition, and we too can leap for joy. Sheila is determined to live in joy and leave a legacy, one her daughter, Chloe, can dance to.

We each decide how we will live out the days assigned to us. But sometimes we have to listen hard to hear the music.

A few years ago I stepped off an airplane and fell headlong into a cavern of depression. I had been in a long-term busy schedule that left me no time to brush up on my dance steps. Occasionally I would tell others I was exhausted. I guess I hoped my listeners would rescue me from my demanding pace. But to be honest, I had a habit of whining about one thing or another, and those closest to me had tuned it out long ago. I'm sure I sounded like a radio station that was broadcasting through heavy static.

I'm grateful that a counselor saw I was in real trouble and intervened because by then I was too depressed to help myself. The only music I heard sounded like a dirge. With the assistance of others I cleared my short-term schedule, lightened my future one, and then I rested. It took a couple of months before I could hear a few notes of joy. By month three I even began to twirl a little. The boogie-woogie came later.

I realize, as I look back, that I wanted others to be responsible for important decisions in my life. I didn't want to cut back and disappoint anyone even at the expense of my well-being and my joy. And believe me, when I did cut my schedule, some people were put out. I had to forgive myself for making the mistake of taking on too much, and I had to allow others to be unhappy with my decision to cut back. That's not easy for those of us who have sympathetic natures and who tend to absorb guilt like a dry sponge in a sinkful of water. It is, however, a lesson in humanity and humility.

I confess I still have a tendency to take on a ton of commitments, but I have learned a few important lessons: I am ultimately responsible for my decisions, but I'm human, and I will make mistakes. I also have noted that Jesus sings joy into a listening heart, which means sometimes I need to lay aside even my ballet slippers and be still if I'm to hear His song. Then, when I stand to dance, I'll know the words to the music and be able to jeté for joy.

Isn't that right, Sheila and Shirley?

STEPPING INTO JOY

You will show me the path of life; in Your presence is fullness of joy; at Your right hand are pleasures forevermore. (Psalm 16:11)

Weeping may endure for a night, but joy comes in the morning. (Psalm 30:5)

Your words were found, and I ate them, and Your word was to me the joy and rejoicing of my heart. (Jeremiah 15:16)

"Jesus . . . a song in a word." —Charles Spurgeon

SHOESTRINGS: TYING UP JOY

Jesus, Your name is a holy chorus that stills and focuses the human heart. Please quiet the clanging cymbals of life's demands that clatter in our minds. Refill us with joyous sounds of Your voice. One word from You, Lord, and the lame leap, the crippled pirouette, and those bowed down rise to stand on tiptoes. We are at times lame with limitations, crippled with cares, and bowed down with life's heaviness. We long for Your dance-producing presence and wait for the dawn of joy within us. Amen.

Peace is like fur-lined boots that help us slog through the winters of our lives.

Boots

PEACE

When Les announced he was going mountain climbing, he looked like a boy who had found a humdinger of a slingshot. We were guests at a retreat gathering, and while I was busy doing girl stuff, Les planned to tackle the Camelback Mountains that jutted up behind the hotel. With a grin the girth of Texas, he strutted out the door in his cowboy boots.

Three hours later Les returned, but his grin had turned grim. He looked as though his new slingshot backfired, causing his strut to turn into a hobble. Les grimaced his way across the room, eased himself down on the bed, and began the tenuous chore of extricating his blistered feet from his stylish boots.

Boots are wonderful, but the right boots for the right task are imperative . . . ask Les. Had he bounded out to tackle the rocky trail in mountain boots, he probably still would be kicking stones and enjoying the views. But men so love to conquer, and cowboy boots tend to bring out the John Wayne in them. Yee-haw!

Les said he made it as far as the Praying Monk (a rock formation) when he felt motivated by his pain to join the craggy priest kneeling in prayer. All John Wayne-ness had fizzled in Les. He prayed a parachute would fall from the heavens because my ex-cowboy couldn't imagine descending the mountainside on his throbbing, burning feet.

I understand Les's response to pray. I find pain nudges us—actually shoves us—to deepen our prayer life. When we hurt, we long to be rescued and to be reassured of the Lord's presence. We want the peace that passes understanding, that kid-glove, protective, heart-quieting peace.

While peace can be as comfy as kid-glove boots, peace is also textured like rain boots. Les and I can vouch for that. Some years ago we were stuck in some stormy relational squabbles we couldn't get past until we sought a counselor. She taught us how to step out of the lightning and thunder of our temperaments and to take refuge together under an umbrella of peace talks. This allowed us the objectivity to do some boot wading through old life patterns and to bring closure to hurt feelings. Facing truth and making changes were scary at first, like deliberately stepping into a tempest, but they brought lasting, peaceful solutions, even when the resolution on certain matters was to agree to disagree.

Sometimes peace can feel as if we're tugging on a pair of rugged combat boots, which then requires us to show up for duty. At times life can be severe, people can be oppositional, and circumstances can be devastating. What's a girl to do? If we pull up our toughness, people are offended and we're tagged with indelicate titles like "tough old broad."

Slowly I've slipped into the comfortable boot of realizing I don't have to become angry to make a point and sometimes, actually many times, I don't even need to make a point (see Exodus 14:14). Trust me, this was a revelation.

Sometimes I should speak up, but when I do so,

I should speak with God's peace directing me, which allows me to maintain personal dignity with truth. Peace also acts as a buffer so that truth isn't purposely cruel to the hearer. As a matter of fact, I once overheard someone say, "Truth without compassion is brutality."

I find it impossible to speak severely when my heart is ruled by peace. Now, I confess I'm not fond of being tempered so often my greatest battle is with myself, which is why I need the combat attire of peace to boot me in the right direction. Along with that, I need to remember that if another person is ranting, I don't have to mirror him or her, but I can choose to reflect Christ. Sister Elizabeth Kenny stated, "He who angers you conquers you." Ruminate on that for a while. I did, and I realized I needed to battle less and pray more.

I spoke at a conference on holding our tongue and allowing God to fight more of our battles when a young woman approached me. She held out her index finger for me to see, well, actually to read. Written across her finger were two words, words meant as a reminder when her mouth sped ahead of her good judgment and her finger wagged with accusation: "Shut up."

"Blessed are the peacemakers" is a blessing bestowed on those soldiers who have humbled themselves before the Lord and are willing, if necessary, to slip into combat gear and take marching orders from Him. Just remember this: Scriptural peacemaking isn't giving in to pacify people because we're scared of their reactions or because we just don't want the hassle of dealing with them. No, a true peacemaker's motivation is to glorify God, whether He asks us to speak up or shut up.

Besides combat boots, a pair of hiking boots should be a staple in every wardrobe since so much of life is hotfooting it from one destination to another across all types of terrain. I have scaled up to a few mountaintops, and I have slid down into more than one deep valley. The views are definitely grander from the mountaintop, but I've noticed we do the majority of our living where the fruit grows in the valley. There's nothing wrong with the valley when we allow Jesus to be our way-maker and our peace-giver.

I stumble and get rocks in my socks when I believe life should be easy and all my views should be expansive and clear. But some seasons come in with challenges that loom like rocky inclines, impairing vision and blocking paths. Learning to relinquish my right to see and to know what's ahead puts me in the position of trusting God's plan. And trust is an open invitation for peace to rule in my heart and mind.

Peace is also like fur-lined boots that help us slog through the winters of our lives. And if you've ever been caught in a blizzard without the protection of snow boots, you know how important they are for long-term survival.

The thing about peace, like so many godly attributes, is it shows up best in crisis. For instance, last year the icy winds of grief struck a family in our community, and even though they were heartbroken, they seemed to be warmed by peace, the peace that makes no sense aside from God's compassionate provision. Their ability to move through—not escape or deny—their grief with an inner strength and quietness was as striking as a freshly tunneled path through a formidable snowdrift. We were grateful to see them comforted, and we also were encouraged knowing that when winter winds blow through our home (which they will) we too can know God's peace amidst our loss. It was as if God's peace in others' lives cut a path of hope for us all.

"May the God of hope fill you with all joy and

peace in believing, that you may abound in hope by the power of the Holy Spirit" (Romans 15:13).

STEPPING INTO PEACE

I will give peace in the land, and you shall lie down, and none will make you afraid. (Leviticus 26:6)

Depart from evil and do good; seek peace and pursue it. (Psalm 34:14)

Peace I leave with you, My peace I give to you; not as the world gives do I give to you. Let not your heart be troubled, neither let it be afraid. (John 14:27)

SHOESTRINGS: TYING UP PEACE

Lord, thank You for Your peace lest the strife and dissention in this world permanently rip us asunder. Make us combat-ready with steady hearts. May we not fear the storm or the storm troopers. Press Your marching orders into our minds, and fill us with Your perfect peace that we might have the courage to face life with sanity and dignity. Amen.

Just stop the ticking clock and allow me to catch up, to loaf in my loafers.

Loafers

PATIENCE

For me, loafers mean kick-back times. Not like hammock swinging or bon-bon popping, but a reprieve from airports, security lines, hotels, and speaking platforms. I need a change of pace even if that translates into catching up on household duties and running errands. I consider it a break to shop, organize my closet, clear my desk, restock the pantry, try out a new recipe, or catch up with friends.

The only problem with shifting gears is my impatience. Actually, whether I'm changing from my heels to my loafers or from my house slippers to my sneakers, I can hear Big Ben ticking. Internally I feel as though I'm always on a time clock. I've set the clock, and just between us, I think I may have wound it too tight. But here's the kicker: The more impatient I am with myself, the more ticked I am with others.

Do sales clerks purposely function in slow motion? Are checkout lines longer these days? Do all shopping carts wobble? Why do simple tasks frequently turn complex? And why do traffic lights last so cotton-pickin' long?

These telltale complaints indicate a pressurized personality. I should know. Tick, tick, tick.

My kindred buddy, the racing rabbit of Alice in Wonderland fame, blurted my theme song when he chattered:

I'm late, I'm late, for a very important date
No time to say hello, goodbye,
I'm late, I'm late, I'm late.

And do you remember how grumpy that Hurried Hare always seemed, with nary a smile on his thin lips? One thing for sure: He didn't need a double mocha frappachino.

Some mornings I wake up feeling tardy. What's that about? And the more I try to manage my wispy minutes, the more they seem to escape me. I feel like the British poet Ralph Hodgson when he wrote:

Time, you old gypsy man,
Will you not stay?
Put up your caravan
Just for one day?

Yes, exactly! Just stop the ticking clock and allow me to catch up, to loaf in my loafers.

Since that isn't likely to happen, I stuff my days too full, trying to make up for lost time, which only makes me cranky from my self-inflicted demands. Some days are filled with unavoidable responsibilities, but other days, when I could shift into park, I find myself accelerating anyway. Knee-jerk response perhaps? And who pays for that? Me. And oh, yes, anyone who crosses my motorized loafers.

The other day I was darting through the house looking for my purse. It is terminally elusive. I was late for an appointment, and then the telephone rang. I performed a midair pivot to grab the phone— only it wasn't on its cradle. I could hear it ringing, but I couldn't find it until finally I stumbled on it wedged in the couch's crevices. I grabbed it up just before it stopped its annoying jingle only to be greeted by a syrupy saleswoman. Talk about annoying. I confess my response to her wouldn't have won me the Miss Congeniality award.

I wonder if age causes a gal to run rampant? Maybe I think my sand is sifting too quickly in my hourglass, and I'm trying to outrun the streaming granules. Maybe my temperament is to blame—it's just how I'm wired. Or maybe it's societal pressure. What about hormones? Too many, not enough? Or maybe it's habit. Or maybe, just maybe, in the midst of all this flurry, I need to deliberately put on the brakes.

Put on the brakes was what I should have done sooner last week. I was darting around town trying to do too many things, when I backed out of my parking space and smacked my PT Cruiser into a bruiser of a utility vehicle parked beside me. I'm still not sure how I did it, but $440 later I'm once again reminded I need to slow down.

"He leadeth me beside the still waters" (Psalm 23:2 KJV). Let's see, how long has it been since I allowed the Good Shepherd to guide me to a quiet resting place? For that's where He gives my disheveled interior a semblance of order. That's where my daily priorities take on an eternal perspective. That's where my loud demands acquiesce to His loving presence. And that's where my hurry-up emotions heal.

When I move from the sanctuary of silence back into the windstorm of our world, I find myself valuing people more than my personal agendas. I seem to have a longer wick and instead of flaring up at delays and inconveniences, I remember that my reactions are a way to show forth the Lord's light in a dark and frantic world. And after still-water time, my internal clock moves with sane purpose instead of ticking off my tired emotions.

Impatience breeds ill will while patience illuminates God's will. And this was a news flash for me: God doesn't wear a watch. I offered to get Him one but He didn't seem impressed. Now, that concerned me at first until I considered His track record—He hasn't been late yet! I giggled when I thought of a book title I saw, *God's Never Failed Me, but He's Sure Scared Me to Death a Few Times.*

Loafers help us to make our way through the cobblestone path of life, and the Lord helps us to patiently survive the trip. So if you, like me, become overwound and feel ready to pop your mainspring, join me as we step out of the frenzy and into His quiet refuge.

STEPPING INTO PATIENCE

Count it all joy when you fall into various trials, knowing that the testing of your faith produces patience. (James 1:2–3)

But the ones [seeds] that fell on the good ground are those who, having heard the word with a noble and good heart, keep it and bear fruit with patience. (Luke 8:15)

Now may the God of patience and comfort grant you to be like-minded toward one another, according to Christ Jesus, that you may with one mind and one mouth glorify the God and Father of our Lord Jesus Christ. (Romans 15:5–6)

SHOESTRINGS: TYING UP JOY

Lord, even as I ask that You would make us more patient, I want to add . . . please hurry. What is all this hurriedness about? Remove the churning from our pace. Slow us down. We don't want to rush past the purpose of life's trials and lose their wealth. Nor do we want to miss the sweetness of Your presence in still moments. Release us from our pressurized personalities. Plant the seeds of patience within our lives that we might grow into graciousness. And thank You for Your patience toward us when we are slow to learn but quick to act. Help us to reflect Your graciousness toward ourselves and toward others. Amen.

Had I been Moses, my tendency, when the people were sarcastic, would be to draw up my intimidating self to my full stature—all five feet—and to bellow, "Jump back, Jack. I'm in charge here!"

Sandals

KINDNESS

$\mathcal{A}$iry—that's how I'd describe a sandal. Definitely not designed for, say, a Michigan winter. Les is from the top of the Upper Peninsula of Michigan, snow country where an average of two hundred and sixty inches of the white stuff falls per year. When people ask him what summer is like up there he tells them, "On that day we would play baseball." Or as one sage described the weather, "They have nine months of winter and three months of bad sledding." Any way you word it, it's cold. So I don't think you would do a big sandal business in them thar parts. Oops, my southern heritage is showing.

My kin are from Kentucky, a state full of blue-grass, horses, hats, and sandals. Actually many

Kentuckian youngsters go barefoot during the summer, but my northern upbringing made me a tenderfoot. I'm a fair-skinned, blue-eyed blonde so I scorch easily. I found the heat and humidity of the South required a well-aerated shoe or your foot would melt into the rubber sole, and the sole would be absorbed into the hot cement, turning you into a permanent tattoo on the sidewalk. I know I've spent many a summer vacation under the sweltering southern sun with my sneakers oozing mushy rubber. I should have worn sandals.

The Israelites knew that was the preferred footwear, as they hiked across the sweltering desert. Imagine if they had worn high tops.

Shoes in Bible times were never worn indoors so putting on sandals, a piece of leather tied onto the foot, was a sign of readiness for activity. Moses led the active sandal parade for forty years. When his people stepped out of Egypt and into the wilderness, they had no idea how long they would have to walk or how far. They also didn't know how hot their feet would be before it was over.

Egyptians drew pictures of their enemies on their shoes' soles so they could literally walk on their foes. Maybe the Israelites should have followed suit; then they might not have minded their long walk and hot tootsies, knowing they had the bad guys underfoot. Instead, the perilous journey made the children of Israel downright cranky.

While I'm not drawn to hot sands or long walks, I would have thought the Israelites would have been grateful that their sandals held up. Mine last a summer if I'm fortunate while theirs lasted forty years. Now that's workmanship. I'd like to meet their cobbler.

I've always admired Moses' kind heart and servant's spirit that he displayed as the Israelites' sandal-clad desert guide. He showed forbearance with a people who majored in murmuring at every mishap they suffered. If you've ever traveled with a complainer, you know how draining that can be: Are we there yet? . . . It's too hot! . . . I'm hungry . . . Where'd that guy gets his camel's license? . . . Do you have to hit every bump in the road?

When the Israelites hit the Red Sea with the Egyptians hotfooting it after them, the Israelites couldn't find a way of escape so they turned on Moses. They accused him of bringing them out there to die. And then they suggested that maybe

Moses didn't think there was enough real estate in Egypt to bury them. Do you detect sarcasm?

Had I been Moses, my tendency, when the people were sarcastic, would be to draw up my intimidating self to my full stature—all five feet—and to bellow, "Jump back, Jack. I'm in charge here!" Which is why I'm sure my name isn't on God's Rolodex for potential desert guides. No, I'm afraid I'd be the gal at the back of the caravan hauling water (or the pooper scooper) for the camels.

Moses' reaction to their criticism caught my attention. He didn't become defensive, and he didn't boomerang their sarcasm. Instead he announced, "Do not fear!" Moses looked past their attitude and past their words to see their behavior for what it was—knee-knocking fear. He then comforted them, promising that they would see the Lord's salvation that very day. His people were afraid, and I would have been too with the enemy pressing in and with my back against the Red Sea.

Listen to what Moses tells them next: "God will fight for you." What a sage, what a servant. It almost never fails that when I meet a true servant that person, like Moses, exudes kindness.

Don't you love kind people? Around them I feel

safe enough to share my heart, to make a mistake or even to fail miserably. They don't seem to have anything to prove. Or any need to make me feel inferior. Or any need to fix me. What a relief they are from the breakneck pace of society and what a relief to our whiplashed minds. Just being in their company lowers one's blood pressure. In the presence of kindness we feel as if we can step out of life's harshness and enjoy a temporary reprieve.

I wonder if that's how Naomi felt when, in her torrents of grief over the death of her husband and sons, her sandal-clad daughter-in-law Ruth joined her in her journey back to Naomi's home. Ruth heaped kindnesses upon her mother-in-law even as Ruth dealt with her own multiple losses of husband, family, and homeland. How selfless and how like a servant to overflow with concern for others. And later isn't it interesting that, when the man Boaz fell in love with the young widow Ruth, he sealed the transaction for her hand with his shoe (a sandal was a simple form of earnest money). Boaz was wealthy so I wonder if his sandal was a Gucci. Probably not.

I do have to say that sometimes kindness can be hazardous. Take the woman who recently offered to let me squeeze into a hotel elevator in her place. Plenty of people had jammed into the elevator going up, but I saw a tiny spot that I figured I could squish myself into. But I had to move fast. What I didn't realize was that, as I hurriedly passed the kind lady, my purse strap hooked over the hangers from which her clothes draped over her arm. As I dashed, I dragged her and her clothes twenty feet before someone stopped me. I hadn't felt the weight of the collection I had dangling from my purse strap because the woman was running as fast as she could while she tried to disengage. But she was laughing so hard she couldn't yell "stop." Her face and neck were flashing red from the shuffle. Talk about whisking someone off her feet . . . and all she did was be kind.

Recently my friend Sheila extended a cup of kindness to me when she heard I was going to visit my mom and sister. My sister, Elizabeth, who is recovering from a mastectomy, serves as the full-time caregiver for our mom. Our eighty-seven-year-old, 4'10", ninety-pound mother has Alzheimer's and Parkinson's. Her sparrowlike body is frail and bent, her hearing is hopelessly muffled, and her mind is deeply shadowed. She recognizes no one. Elizabeth warned me that Mom had declined since I last saw her and that I should prepare myself.

I asked Sheila to pray for me. I was tired from a busy year of travel, and I was feeling emotionally fragile. I didn't know how I would handle seeing Mom so diminished. My caring friend answered my prayer request with an e-mail that contained these words:

> Sweet face so worn and tired now
> A distant smile of days long gone
> Tread lightly all around her now
> This princess almost wears her crown.
> —Sheila Walsh

I carried that poem with me and reread it many times. While seeing my mom wasn't easy, I was comforted and newly reminded that this diminutive servant was one step away from her crown.

Thank you, Sheila, for helping me in such a gracious manner to remember that, while we see our loved one reduced to a tiny sack of helpless bones, the Lord sees a princess and awaits her entrance into the palace. How divinely kind!

Does your kindness cup runneth over? Are people grateful when they see you approach? Can they trust your heart with their fears and foibles? Are your words saturated in kindness? Are you a servant? How do you respond to sarcasm or criticism?

I just tried answering those questions, and I'm not certain I passed. I think kindness may take time . . . I just hope it's not forty years in the desert.

Hmm . . . better pack my sandals.

STEPPING INTO KINDNESS

She opens her mouth with wisdom, and on her tongue is the law of kindness. (Proverbs 31:26)

Put on tender mercies, kindness, humility, meekness, long-suffering. (Colossians 3:12)

But when the kindness and the love of God our Savior toward man appeared, not by works of righteousness which we have done, but according to His mercy He saved us. (Titus 3:4-5)

SHOESTRINGS: TYING UP KINDNESS

Lord, at times life batters us with rejection, losses, and mis-understandings, causing our hearts to withdraw. Restore our willingness to be tender. Dissolve any hardness in our hearts with Your compassion. May we not hesitate to slip into servant's sandals and run to do Your kind bidding, whether that be overlooking people's behavior when they are sarcastic or comforting others when our own hearts are aching. Fill our kindness cups to overflowing. Amen.

A flip-flop is like a slipper with the top down, and what's more fun than a convertible on a summer's day?

Flip-Flops

GOODNESS

I love a flip-flop day, don't you? When I don these slaphappy shoes, I might be off for a pedicure, a visit to a poolside lounge chair, a jaunt to the garden to gather a quick bouquet, or a cruise to some sun-splashed destination (yes!).

I love flip-flops' instant availability and their wash-and-wear attitude. A flip-flop is like a slipper with the top down, and what's more fun than a convertible on a summer's day? Their casual approach suggests ease and relaxation. Even their slapping rhythm resonates with images of crowded beaches, the distant laughter of children, striped umbrellas under cloudless skies, and frosty tumblers brimming with fresh-squeezed lemonade.

I bet whoever wrote "The best things in life are free" was wearing flip-flops and sunscreen when he penned it. The kicked-back pace of a flip-flop day, week, or vacation allows us to contemplate our blessings. Those hours when we settle in to listen to the diminutive sparrow's soprano lilt, to trace a paunchy bee's zigzag path as it gads about, or to take a stroll through a park unaware of the hour. In those private moments when we hear our heart sigh and let go of the accumulated stress, we begin to celebrate what a wondrous world we live in and recognize that, yes, we are living the good life.

In our society the word *good* is equated with average and common. It seldom generates applause and rates only two to three stars out of a possible five. Yet when we consider some of the ways *good* has been used, we realize this underrated word bursts with righteous satisfaction and deserves our consideration.

In Genesis after Father God designed the lights in the heavens (sun, moon, and stars), He bestowed his five-star seal of approval with, "It is good." Again and again after He inspects some portion of His creation, He breathes "good" over it. From the tip of the highest mountain peak to the depth of the valley floor, from the tip of the tallest red-wood to its deepest buried root, from the tip of our head to the soles of our feet, He proclaims, "Good, good, good."

Goodness reverberates with purity, wholesome-ness, and at its core, excellence. Good doesn't emerge out of bad unless God's redeeming hand is involved—He who is goodness itself. That's why John the Baptist described Jesus this way: "There comes One after me who is mightier than I, whose sandal strap I am not worthy to stoop down and loose" (Mark 1:7). The Lord speaks good into calamity to redeem and deepen His children's lives. After humankind's fall He was willing to work goodness into our flawed characters and our sin-smudged motives.

Sometimes we say, "I feel good about myself" after we have chosen an honorable path. No superlatives, no adjectives are necessary to pump added meaning or to spit-shine our behavior for company. "Good's" clear ring resounds throughout our beings, declaring that, when we make right choices, we're satisfied with the word's simple integrity.

I recently met a woman doctor from India who is working with AIDS patients in her country. She was told of a woman who as a child had been sold onto the streets to make money as a prostitute. She is now a young woman in the last throes of AIDS and has been relegated to a small room in her family's home. Not even her relatives go near her. Once a day she is slid a plate of food and then left to sit alone to wait for death. The first thing the doctor did upon her arrival at that home was to touch and stroke the patient's arm.

To me, this doctor's outstretched hand was a powerful picture of goodness. No hidden agenda, nothing to gain, just a heart willing to give a suffering person a tender connection and to help to restore the woman's dignity.

I once read a poem that began, "We shall walk in velvet shoes." That line rang with goodness for me, and I thought of the doctor's soft footsteps, going in and out of others' lives, bringing healing, comfort, kindness, and tenderness. I had a feeling that when God saw the doctor's hand on that forsaken woman, He proclaimed in the heavens, "It is good."

I wonder if velvet flip-flops exist. I've observed jeweled, iridescent, and transparent ones, but I don't remember ever seeing velvet. I'd like some as a reminder that even in my time off from my labors I'm called to walk in goodness.

Do you think under her habit Mother Teresa wore velvet flip-flops? She certainly left footprints of goodness all over the world, whether she was "at work" in Calcutta hovering over the dying, at the White House representing the world's needy, or in her morning and evening "time off," presenting herself in prayer to the Lord.

Christianity has no time clock; we don't get to clock out. Our faith is a full-time calling, whether we've donned jeans and flip-flops or our evening dress with beaded heels. We can be on our knees at church, weeding a garden, or extracting a splinter from a toddler's finger, and it's all part of our good calling.

My friend Carol is an artist and travels regularly doing shows. Even though her work demands constant involvement, she is sensitive to an even higher calling, that of grandmother. Recently her grandson Randy turned ten years old while he was away at muscular dystrophy camp. His wheelchair-bound body requires others' help to make his life more tolerable. Carol, behind in last-minute preparations for an art show the following day, set aside her work, put on her flip-flops, and made a beeline to the camp where she became Randy's hands and legs. She hauled what felt like a lakeful of water one bucket at a time to fill a leaky moat around a sandcastle she had designed for her darling grandson. Randy was the presiding king over the castle, giving his serf-grandma instructions on what he wanted. She returned home exhausted, behind in her art, and feeling good about her choice.

We can easily allow the immediate to rob us of the eternal. Our daily agendas sometimes carry us along like a fast-moving stream, and we forget we can grab a limb, rudder our canoe, and either get out and take the path or paddle upstream. Going against the current isn't easy, but sometimes it's necessary if we're to end up where we belong and not become victims of our own calendars.

Speaking of calendars, as I write we're in June. We all know that traditionally that means graduations and weddings, a monthful of celebrations. I've learned that often the shoe of choice for both is, yep, flip-flops. Who would have guessed? That simple shoe is making fashion history with its unexpected versatility (maybe velvet ones really do exist). Still, regardless what fancy footwear we don, it's what path we trod, even if we do it barefoot, that counts.

STEPPING INTO GOODNESS

May your saints rejoice in your goodness. (2 Chronicles 6:41 NIV)

I am still confident of this: I will see the goodness of the LORD in the land of the living. (Psalm 27:13 NIV)

But you, O Sovereign LORD, deal well with me for your name's sake; out of the goodness of your love, deliver me. (Psalm 109:21 NIV)

How can I repay the LORD for all his goodness to me? (Psalm 116:12 NIV)

SHOESTRINGS: TYING UP GOODNESS

You, Lord, and only You are good. Your generous love allows us to experience Your goodness and to share it with others. The purity of goodness is like a crystal stream in which You invite us to kneel and drink deeply. May we not sully Your offering by assuming our trite efforts are enough without the purging Your goodness accomplishes in our motives and character. We rejoice in You. Amen.

I mean, who designed high heels anyway?
A contortionist? They hurt my back,
my feet, and my feelings.

High Heels

FAITHFULNESS

I'm five feet tall and shrinking. I can't afford this kind of loss; as it is, I need all the assistance I can get to see over counters, people's heads, and lecterns. Since childhood I've required ladders of one sort or another: telephone books, stools, crates, and risers. I understand that one of Japan's emperors for his coronation (in the 1920s) wore twelve-inch heels called *getas*. I wonder if he loans those out? Now, well into my adult life, I, like the emperor, have found high heels give me a definite boost.

But here's my challenge: The older I get the less able I am to endure my head in the clouds. Actually, it's not so much the position of my head as the condition of my feet. I mean, who designed high heels anyway? A contortionist? They hurt my back, my feet, and my feelings. They even cause me to have charley horses. Yikes! Those electrical leg knots hurt! Someone once said, "The best way to forget all your troubles is to wear tight shoes." I'd like to add that high heels can do the job just as well.

Yet without high heels I need a neck brace to look up at everybody. I sure can't tote telephone books around, strap a crate to my back, or like Zacchaeus search for a nearby sycamore tree (see Luke 19:3–4). So when I need added inches, high heels give me the needed boost up into the rest of the world.

A few years back I spoke at, of all places, the Final Four basketball championship playoffs for some of the coaches' wives. Can you picture me, the Lilliputian, milling around the giants of sportsdom? Every time I left my room and ventured into the elevators or lobby, I was staring at basketball players' kneecaps. I felt as if I were in the featured role for *Oops, We Shrunk the Speaker*.

Even sporting my highest heels, I wasn't on speaking terms with those guys. We're talking vertically extreme meets vertically challenged. I'm grateful that, while I'm insignificant, there is One who has reached down from the heavens to lift me up. One who converses with me at a moment's notice and who has promised never to leave or forsake me. And while I'm sure the basketball players who rode with me that day in the elevators didn't mean to ignore my presence, they did. (Actually, they never even noticed me down yonder standing guard over their shoe tops.) In contrast, the Lord is aware of every sigh of my heart, and He comforts my aches and my pains. He who is high and lifted up (no riser or Reeboks required) is faithful . . . even to little old me.

Faithfulness is a wondrous attribute. It's all about reliability, steadiness, firmness, and supportiveness. Our God holds steady when we're standing tall and when we take a foolish fall. We can be in our worst mood or on our Sunday-best behavior; yet He remains trustworthy.

I used to believe God loved me as long as I behaved. Oh, I don't think I ever verbalized that as my belief, but I certainly behaved as though it was true. Problem was I couldn't behave. Then one day, like a lantern being lit in a cave, it came to me that in the midst of my worst behavior Christ wooed me into His love. And if He could love me as raucous as I was then, I could trust Him to be faithful and love me through till glory. His acceptance of us isn't based on our behavior but on His unchanging love.

As a child my parents took me to the Mammoth Caves in Kentucky, touted as the world's longest cave system. During the tour, the adults were amazed by the surroundings. But I was unimpressed with this eerie underground world and just wanted back in the sunlight where I could see the sky.

I was to repeat that journey as a young adult— only not to the Mammoth Caves but to a mammoth pit called depression. For several years I lived in an eerie world of anxiety attacks, anger, and sadness. No heels were high enough to lift me above my misery. My fervent prayer was that I might somehow make it back into the sunlight of life.

My journey was slow, like one inching across a high wire in heels. But when a person realizes she is fighting for her life, speed doesn't matter, just progress and survival. Again and again the Lord lifted my sagging spirit with lanterns of truth and set me on solid ground. I often proclaimed with

David, "He also brought me up out of a horrible pit, out of the miry clay, and set my feet upon a rock, and established my steps" (Psalm 40:2).

I love the word "also" in that text. It alerts us that this is just one of the things God did for David. I was a multimedia project, and I appreciated the reassurance that the Lord would be with me despite my layers of brokenness, that He would do a lot of "alsos" for me. I'm humbled that He takes on high-maintenance children.

And don't miss the word "up" in that verse. A wee word chock-full of explosive hope that proclaims, yes, an end will come to the down days. In the midst of our struggles, we feel as if the pain will be eternal, but in truth most situations are fleeting.

I'm often asked how long it took me to step out from under the spirit of heaviness that covered me. My healing felt gradual yet ongoing. I was in a much bigger hurry for my liberation than God seemed to be. I wanted to leap into freedom while He encouraged me step by step. We like timelines so we can set our clocks for our recovery, but God, unimpeded and unimpressed by our digital sundials, continues to work individually and faithfully to complete His work in us. We can rest assured.

So whether you're standing heads above the crowd or you're feeling helpless and small in the darkest pit, there is One who will assist you in taking the next step. Why? Because He is faithful to do what He has promised.

STEPPING INTO FAITHFULNESS

It is good to give thanks to the LORD, and to sing praises to Your name, O Most High; to declare Your lovingkindness in the morning, and Your faithfulness every night. (Psalm 92:1–2)

Through the LORD's mercies we are not consumed, because His compassions fail not. They are new every morning; great is Your faithfulness. (Lamentations 3:22–23)

Your faithfulness endures to all generations; You established the earth, and it abides. (Psalm 119:90)

SHOESTRINGS: TYING UP FAITHFULNESS

What a relief to know we can rely on You, O Lord. It causes us to breathe more deeply, sleep more soundly, choose more selectively, love more unselfishly, and live more sanely. Your steadfast nature gives us a sense of belonging and rootedness. You are our Night Watchman and our Day Guard, assuring us of Your ongoing presence. Morning by morning we are renewed by Your enduring, faithful ways. Amen.

Gentle people enter our lives like a welcome breeze and leave without slamming the door.

Slippers

GENTLENESS

On nippy October evenings, just give me a crackling fireplace, a cup of cocoa (extra marshmallows please), and my time-worn slippers. Then I'll purr like a kitten with catnip. Blustery outside, toasty inside—that's the cozy environment for watching a movie, lingering over a well-written article, or entering into meaningful dialogue. My house slippers add the snuggle factor and are imperative to the evening's success. Besides, after especially aerobic days, my barking dogs need the gentle housing of a slipper.

I just counted, and I own seven pairs of house slippers—fat ones, fancy ones, furry ones, and some fun ones. I know seven is a lot, but some were gifts and a few are still in their original packaging (old people do that, you know). I favor one well-trodden pair. In fact, you could probably lift a clear footprint from my brown slippers since I've been scooting around in them for years; they look like a science project gone awry. I wouldn't risk putting them under a microscope for a critter count. Yet when I arrive home and catch a glimpse of their crumpled, fuzzy form, I begin to relax.

House slippers are comforting, probably because they aren't restrictive and their expectations of me are minimal—with the exception of my black-and-white-spotted cow slippers. They make me feel as if I should burst into a round of clogging. Oh yeah, I once had a pair of embroidered Swiss slippers with tiny tinkling bells on them. Les gave them away because every time I slipped them on, I would yodel.

House slippers are generally devoid of shoestrings, buckles, heavy heels, and other encumbrances. I appreciate the gentle design of hospitable slippers.

I have friends like that, ones with a gentle design. When I catch a glimpse of these gal pals, their very presence is like a warm hug or a loving pat of affirmation. My blood pressure lowers in their nurturing company. I feel accepted by them, which eliminates the rigors of doing handstands to try to prove myself or performing plate-twirling feats to gain their attention. Their expectations of me are minimal because they trust God will handle me. And, get this—gentle friends like me, even when I'm decked out in my bed-head, tattered housecoat, and matted slippers. Now that's impressive.

A relative quipped recently upon seeing my morning appearance, "Say, you're kind of scary-looking." Thank you for mentioning it. Years ago I answered the door in my housecoat decked out with rollers (remember those?) and face cream, and the startled salesman remarked, "Oh, I'm sorry. It's obvious that you're not feeling well. I'll come back another time." Hmm, too bad that doesn't work with telemarketers.

Gentle people are important to society. Gentle people are important to my life. They soften life's harsh edges (and mine), they add sweetness to bitter circumstances, and they ease the biting winds of loss. Gentle people enter our lives like a welcome breeze and leave without slamming the door.

My friend Ney Bailey is like that. She joins the

Women of Faith group from time to time, and our entire staff lights up when we see her. Ney stays in the background, emerging to offer a hand, click a picture, celebrate the good fortune of others, and pray for a need. Whatever way Ney can be of service this gentle-breeze, slipper-clad servant is there, and when she leaves, you never even hear the door close behind her.

Now, I'm gusty by nature. I can still hear my mother calling out for the gazillionth time, "Don't slam the door!" Some folks are easygoing while others of us have had to be coached in gentleness by the Holy Spirit.

My son Jason is a gentle soul; even his name means "peacemaker." When he came to work for me, I was concerned people wouldn't take him seriously because he was soft-spoken and non-confrontational. I wondered how he would fare with hotel clerks, cab drivers, and the airlines people. It didn't take long to find out that he garnered better results with his gentle-breeze approach than I did with all my huffing and puffing. I began to take notes.

Jason seems instinctively to know that "a soft answer turns away wrath" (Proverbs 15:1), whereas

I've had to have that truth riveted onto my heart's tablet with a jackhammer. You would think by the time one has her AARP card she would have her mouth figured out. Not only have I had to be tutored in a softer pattern of communication, but I'm also still learning what it means to have a listening ear.

In the Old Testament story of the prophet Elijah, he sought to hear the Lord's voice after a Reebok run for his life, and that voice came in a gentle breeze (and he was strengthened by the whispered communication). In contrast, the whining Israelites filled the desert air with their complaints and didn't hear God's voice until it came crashing down Mt. Sinai in bolts of lightning and rumbling thunder (and it left them weak-kneed and shaking in their sheepskin shorts).

Different strokes for different folks. What does it take to get your attention? While I'm generally a thunder kind of gal, some days I have responded to the gentler moves of His Spirit. I long to do that more frequently, and I suspect that's your desire as well.

I don't think any of us wants to learn all her lessons the hard way, yet I'd have to confess that's the course I've usually taken. When I ran away from home as a rebellious teenager, I wasn't gone a week before I realized I had made a terrible mistake. It may have been the blisters on my knees from kneeling in a potato patch picking spuds as I tried to make some pocket change that convinced me. Too proud to admit my mistake and too immature to change, I added years of poor choices that eventually stockpiled into a guilt-ridden, fear-laden existence. In time I asked the Lord if I could exchange my mucky swamp waders for His slippers of gentleness. He tenderly welcomed me home.

Under the Spirit's tutelage, let's decide to move gingerly (wear house slippers) into and through other's lives, that we might leave a legacy of gentleness. And may we be so attuned to our gentle Savior's voice that we instantly hush in His presence and listen up.

Stepping into Gentleness

I, therefore, the prisoner of the Lord, beseech you to have a walk worthy of the calling with which you were called, with all lowliness and gentleness, with longsuffering, bearing with one another in love, endeavoring to keep the unity of the Spirit in the bond of peace. (Ephesians 4:1-3)

You have also given me the shield of Your salvation; Your right hand has held me up, Your gentleness has made me great. (Psalm 18:35)

Let your gentleness be known to all men. The Lord is at hand. (Philippians 4:5)

SHOESTRINGS: TYING UP GENTLENESS

Gentle Savior, forgive our brash manner when we flurry into Your presence with demands. Teach us to kneel before we petition You, lest we remain insensitive to Your heart. May we learn from the gentleness that surrounds us—the morning breeze, the dove's coo, the snowflake's flutter, the fragrance from a crushed rose petal, the down in a nest. All around us are Your fingerprints of gentleness. May we too leave a gentle imprint on our abrasive society. We all long for the comfort only Your gentle touch can bring. Amen.

*C'mon, let's lace up our
tennis shoes and take a lap.*

Tennis Shoes

SELF-CONTROL

I'm kicking up dust! Note my smoke! I'm sporting sneakers, and I'm making history!

History? Well, *my* history anyway. You see, I've taken up walking. For most of my life a walking regimen hasn't been part of my daily repertoire. About a year ago I tried it out for a while, but alas, the activity eventually drizzled out of my schedule. Then, more recently, I marched back into a bit of a routine. Which is my way of saying my effort is still sporadic, so I confess the dust and smoke intro was a smidge optimistic.

Once I hit the street, though, I can, as the kids say, book. Dragging my reluctant self out there seems to be the holdup. At first I didn't have the correct footwear (one limp around the block proved that), so I invested in a good pair of walking shoes. I didn't like walking alone, but I wasn't ready to commit to walk at a certain time each day either. So how could I find a spontaneous walking buddy? Finally I bought a tape player with headphones to be my on-the-road companion, and voila, I was ready . . . sorta.

Discipline isn't my strongest suit. I wish it was, but I'm aware I have to do more than wish for it— I have to work for it. Hup, two, three, four. I read some years ago that it takes three weeks of consistent effort to establish a new habit. Hup, two, three, four. Until then, we have to consciously push ourselves toward change. Hup, two, three, four.

One shove in the right direction for me was when I discovered a tape of a gal with a convincing voice providing instruction on proper walking techniques. In the background is hip-swinging, foot-stomping music, and after she tells you how to stand, place your feet, breathe, and pace yourself, she leaves you alone with the music to prance with purpose. Since I love music, I can really get into the beat. Although I must admit I'm tempted to stop my forward motion and break dance, but so far I've resisted that urge. Somehow having my back in traction doesn't sound appealing.

I didn't realize I needed someone to tell me how to walk until I listened to this tape. For years I've been slinging one foot in front of the other, thinking that was enough. I mean, I got where I was going. But now I know I could have benefited from a few expert tips.

Actually, Scripture has a lot to say about our walk and our need for self-control. Self-control? You know, the importance of listening to the talk in our heads that convinces us to make better choices. Not the voice that says, "Go ahead, pour a little chocolate over your oatmeal. It will make that goo more tolerable." No, not that voice. Self-control is the voice of personal discipline. It's the one that says, "Honey, you just put enough food on your plate for three starving sumo wrestlers. Wrap up three-quarters of that and send it to the nearest soup kitchen; it will feed their staff." Yep, that's the voice, the nudges of our own personal trainer.

Gaining self-control has much more to do with listening to our brain than to our emotions. Brains are way more reasonable, ever notice that? Emotions, at least mine, are given to spells of feisty fits and frivolous fluctuations. Self-control, from my experience, is taking responsibility for one's responses to life, about exercising choices, and about growing up. Talk about a workout!

I know people hire personal trainers, but I've wondered if that was asking someone else to be in charge of my choices. Now that would be a scary responsibility. I do know we benefit from having an informed cheerleader and mentor in our lives; so perhaps if we linked a human trainer with our self-control that team in tandem would bring about solid results. Eventually, though, we're going to be on our own, and that's when the shoe rubber meets the proverbial road.

I joined a weight program last winter to deal with my holiday gain; somehow the turkey didn't look as inviting hanging like saddlebags off my hips as it had when I served it up on my best porcelain platter. I was shoehorning my body into my clothes.

At the beginning of the program, for ten consecutive days, I ate prescribed minimeals consisting of Styrofoam-tasting morsels, drank gallons of water, and walked faithfully. I didn't cheat, and I didn't even whine (aloud). I was determined to exercise not only my body but also my self-control.

On day ten I went into the center to be weighed, so I wore my lightest weight clothing and brushed the weighty hairspray out of my tresses. Then before stepping on the scale, I removed my watch, earrings, and tennis shoes. I didn't want anything interfering with my success. I stepped onto the unforgiving machine only to hear my weight counselor announce that I had lost three ounces.

"Ounces? Ounces!" I screeched at the pitch of a coyote in labor. "You have to be kidding! I could have shaved my legs and lost three ounces." I was beside myself. The only thing I could think of that might weigh a lousy three ounces was a gnat's elbow or a spider's kneecap. C'mon, three ounces?

Later I realized that since starting the program I not only felt better, but I also had improved my stamina, my fuzzy head seemed clearer, and my jiggly places were toning up. Not to mention the shot in the arm staying on the program was for my self-esteem. (I've found making wise choices is the quickest way to improve a sagging self-esteem.) My efforts were paying off—just not in the way I had imagined.

Self-control means we draw healthy boundaries for our behavior and choices. I'm grateful the Holy

Spirit is our personal trainer, offering counsel and enabling us in the areas of our weakness.

Wanna practice kickin' up dust? C'mon, let's lace up our tennis shoes and take a lap. Hup, two, three, four . . .

STEPPING INTO SELF-CONTROL

But also for this very reason, giving all diligence, add to your faith virtue, to virtue knowledge, to knowledge self-control, to self-control perseverance. (2 Peter 1:5–6)

But know this, that in the last days perilous times will come: For men will be . . . unloving, unforgiving, slanderers, without self-control. (2 Timothy 3:1–3)

Let us walk properly, as in the day, not in revelry and drunkenness, not in lewdness and lust, not in strife and envy. But put on the Lord Jesus Christ, and make no provision for the flesh, to fulfill its lusts. (Romans 13:13–14)

SHOESTRINGS: TYING UP SELF-CONTROL

Lord, left on our own we do things that aren't appropriate, we say things that aren't thoughtful, we react abruptly, and we mindlessly cater to our humanity. Counsel us by Your Spirit. Guide us toward maturity. Draw holy boundaries in iridescent ink on our hearts so we don't miss them. Deliver us from our many addictions and indulgences. May we walk with purposed steps toward You as You teach us the importance of not humoring our "me" but instead worshiping "thee." Amen.

Some of the smallest footprints leave some of the most unforgettable impressions.

Kickin' Up Dust

Hi! I'm Buster Brown.
I live in a shoe.
This is my dog, Tige.
He lives there too.

That was my favorite commercial as a youngster.
Anybody remember it?

Now, my question is, Why did the kid live in a
shoe? Do you think his mother was the Old Lady
who had so many children she didn't know what to
do? Maybe Buster became accustomed to the smell
of leather and was fed up with his many siblings (and
porridge) and moved out on his own. He seemed
like a good kid, clean-cut, personable, and all. Or
maybe the Old Lady expanded her living space, and
Buster and Tige's shoe was an addition on the back
forty. (Smart mom to send the dog with him.)

As much as I like shoes, I don't want to live
inside one. In fact, I appreciate folks who, when

they come to visit, make the friendly gesture of slipping off their shoes at the front door. I'm not a stickler on that, but I've noticed it's easier on my wood floors, especially in the high-traffic areas.

Speaking of high-traffic areas, isn't that a good description of our lives? I mean, how many people enter and exit your life in a year? A hundred? A thousand? And how many lives do you walk in and out of as you circle the globe of your life? That's really what this book has been all about: our walk and our encounters with others.

Left on my own, I find my relationships lacking, which is why I'm grateful for a personal relationship with Christ. He promises via His Word and His Spirit to direct my steps whether that's down a solitary path or one teeming with folks.

Does that mean I now make no relational blunders? Nah. Yet I'm far more able to adjust both internally and externally to family, friends, and newcomers that surround my life than I once was. And when I mess up big-time or even tiny-time, I can go to the Lord in prayer, and He forgives my rash behavior and strengthens my feeble character. He even gives me the courage and words to make things right face to face with my opponent.

People have a way of exposing how well we are laced up internally. Have you noticed that? One yank on our strings, and we can become untied. Our interactions alert us to when our souls need relining, and they even expose when we're acting like out-and-out heels.

The Bible is crowded with wise counsel that can raise the bar of our behavior and improve the quality of our interior lives. Then we will have the space to assimilate truth and relinquish our lives to Christ to walk in love, joy, peace, patience, kindness, goodness, faithfulness, gentleness, and self-control.

Whether our shoes are canvas, silk, brocade, straw, plastic, leather, beaded, wood, cork, lace, suede, or bejeweled, what folks will remember is if, when we walked in their space, we did so respectfully and tenderly, holding dear their personage. Nope, it's not the style of our footwear but the flare (yes, flare, as in light) of our faith. Why, it's not even the size of our feet . . .

I heard a report that a famous athlete sports a size 22 shoe. Wow! That's not a shoe; that's a canoe! The Old Lady should put a bid in on one of those. It would be like living in a high-rise. Of course, she would need to buy stock in an odor-eater company.

Some of the folks I've known, ones who made huge impacts on my life, didn't wear canoes. In fact, quite the opposite. People like my mom, Rebecca, who when she married at the age of nineteen wore a size $2\frac{1}{2}$ shoe. Yep, that's right, a $2\frac{1}{2}$. C'mon, that's not a shoe; that's a kazoo! How would one keep from toppling over with such a miniscule foundation? Yet she was one surefooted woman, especially in her walk of faith.

Today Mom can no longer walk, and Alzheimer's and Parkinson's have hopelessly muddled her thinking. But spiritually she continues to amaze us.

Earlier this year my sister, Elizabeth, was diagnosed with breast cancer. Beth's husband was in Korea on assignment for the Air Force at the time. She was afraid, lonely, and in need of comforting. When she walked into the living area of her home with a heavy heart, Mom called her over to her bedside. Mom calls my sister "Hey, lady," having long ago forgotten her name. Elizabeth leaned over to hear what she wanted when Mom reached up, slipped her arms around Elizabeth's neck, drew her in close, and prayed, "May you know the comfort and strength of the Lord. In Jesus' name, amen."

Elizabeth sobbed.

She told me later, "If ever I needed to hear Mom pray for me, it was then."

Mom had lived with my sister for six years, but during that time she had never prayed aloud for Elizabeth because Mom's progressive diseases had splintered her thoughts. Yet that day, for whatever reason, God ordained our little mom to return mentally just long enough to wrap her youngest adult child in prayer. Now that's flare! Even in her debilitated (crippled, confused, almost deaf) condition the Lord continues to use her. You go, Mom!

Nope, you don't have to lug size 22 shoes around this planet for folks to remember you've been here. A kazoo-size will do. Some of the smallest footprints leave some of the most unforgettable impressions.

Whether we're attending a sandaled tea party, a loafer lunch, a high-heeled reception, a ballet slippered recital, a baby bootie shower, a flip-flopping beach party, or a boot-trudging meeting, may we step into it with a sense of our lasting influence on others. And may we run (tennis shoes) to Christ and rest (slippers) in His presence so that we might walk (flare) worthy of our high calling.

Now get out there and kick up some dust.